D1269453

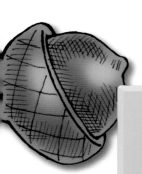

How Many Ways Can You Cut a Pie?

A book about math

BY JANE BELK MONCURE • ILLUSTRATED BY RONNIE ROON

The **Child's World**

Published by The Child's World®
1980 Lookout Drive • Mankato, MN 56003-1705
800-599-READ • www.childsworld.com

Acknowledgments
The Child's World®: Mary Berendes, Publishing Director
The Design Lab: Design
Jody Jensen Shaffer: Editing

ISBN 9781623235796
LCCN 2013931417

Printed in the United States of America
Mankato, MN
July 2013
PA02177

Did you know...

A library is a magic castle with many Word Windows in it?

What is a Word Window?

If you said, "A book," you're right!

A book is a Word Window because the words and pictures let you look and see many things. Books are your windows to the wide, wide world around you.

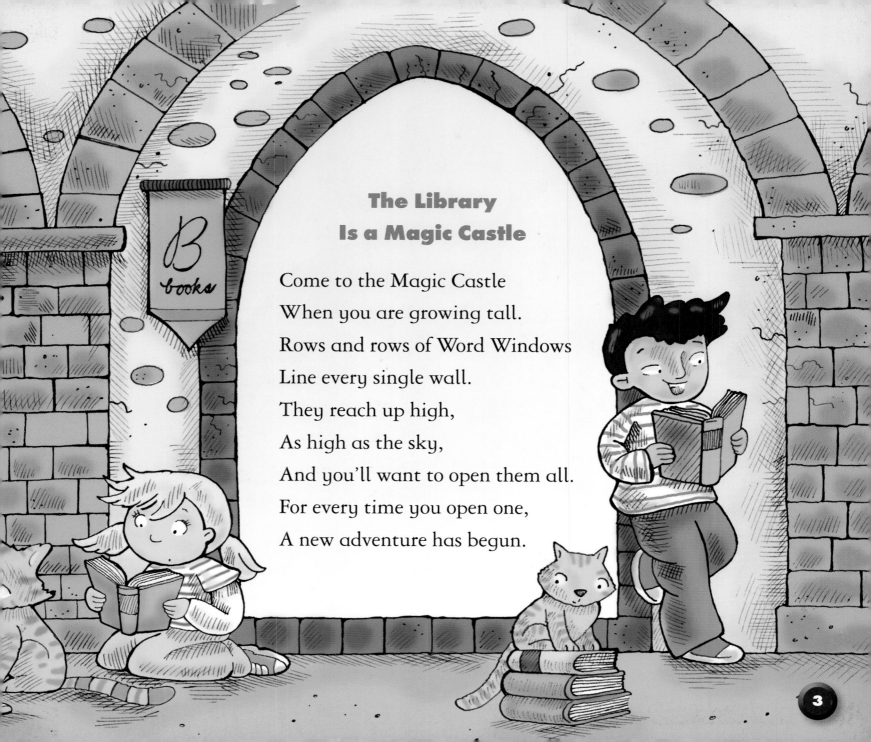

The Library Is a Magic Castle

Come to the Magic Castle
When you are growing tall.
Rows and rows of Word Windows
Line every single wall.
They reach up high,
As high as the sky,
And you'll want to open them all.
For every time you open one,
A new adventure has begun.

Hank opened a Word Window.
Here is what he read:

One fall day, Squirrel saw a sign. It read:
Pie contest today! Signed, Pig.

"I will bake my best acorn pie for the contest," Squirrel said. And she did.

The pie was still hot when Mouse came by.
"My," said Mouse. "What a fine pie."

"Will you cut the pie in two pieces?
One half for me, one half for you?"

"No," said Squirrel. "This pie is for Pig's contest. If I win, I will share my pie with you."

Then Frog came by.
"My," said Frog. "What a fine pie."

"Will you cut the pie into three pieces?
One piece for you, one piece for Mouse,
and one piece for me?"

"No," said Squirrel. "This pie is for Pig's contest.
If I win, I will share my pie with you."

The pie was still hot.
Squirrel put it in the window to cool.

Then the three friends went for a walk
in the woods.

While they were gone, Pig came by.
"My," said Pig. "What a fine pie."

"I will try just one little bite."

"Yum," said Pig.

Then Pig ate another bite.
"This is just right," she said.

Pig ate and ate until she cleaned the plate.

Just then, Squirrel and her friends came home.

"Oh no! Why did you eat my pie?" said Squirrel.

"Was your pie for my pie contest today?"
asked Pig.
"Yes," said Squirrel.

Pig took something out of her pocket.

It was a ribbon for Squirrel.

"Surprise! You win my pie contest!" said Pig.
"Your pie was the very best."

"That is not fair," said Mouse.

"That is not fair at all," said Frog. "You ate the whole pie that we were going to share."

"I did not mean to eat the whole pie," said Pig.
"I will try to make things right."

Pig went outside and found more acorns.

"Squirrel makes the best pies of all," said Pig.
"Maybe she will make one more pie."

Squirrel made one more pie.
She cut it into four pieces.
Everyone had a fair share.

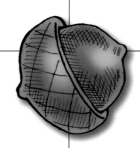

Questions and Activities

(Write your answers on a sheet of paper.)

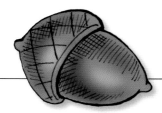

1. Describe two characters in the story.
   Write two things about each one.

2. What do you call the pieces of a pie
   that has been cut into two pieces?

3. Why did Pig give Squirrel a ribbon for her pie?
   Why did Pig not give Frog a ribbon?

4. Did parts of this story make you feel sad or happy? Why?

5. At the end of the story, how many friends were there?
   How many pieces did Squirrel cut the pie into?
   Add the numbers of friends and pieces of pie. How many do you have?